Darean Polk

My Writes
to Freedom

Wider Perspectives Publishing ∞ Norfolk, Va. ∞ 2021

The poems and writings in this book are the creations and property of Darean Polk; the author is responsible for them as such. Wider Perspectives Publishing reserves 1st run rights to this material in this form, all rights revert to author upon delivery. Author's rights reserved: Do not reproduce without permission. Author may redistribute, whole or in part, at will, for example submission to anthologies or contests.

Front Cover Art by Curtis Johnson

Copyright © November 2021, Darean Polk
Wider Perspectives Publishing, Norfolk, Va
ISBN: 978-1-952773-49-5

You can find Darean on Instagram at   writes_to_freedom

Contents

A Word to Boys	1
Ecstasy	4
Bodies	6
Like The Ocean	8
Untitled	9
Pretty Please	11
Underdog	12
The Question & Answer to The Question	14
Separation	16
Hey, It's Our Love Song	17
Hades	19
Nostalgia	21
Poison	23
Mumbo Jumbo	24
Sunflower	26
Reminder: Stay High	27
Inhibition	29
Surrender	30
Perfect, Imperfection	31
Homecoming	32
Forward	34
Just a Kid	35
Freedom	38
The Power of Our Love	39
Finally	41

A Word to Boys

Yo, I don't think it's true that niggas ain't shit
Y'all are not the same, but to the ones I dealt with
You've all broken my heart and it's making me real sick
I hope you slip up and, uhh, suck a dick
I put my heart into those relationships
I love with every fiber of my being
And you were quick to complain and threaten me with leaving
I couldn't believe the change of behavior I was seeing
You wooed me and your words soothed me in the beginning
Your hearts turn to stone and love to dust
Your words became deceiving, I soon lost my trust
Start giving me cold shoulders
I'm like yo what the fuck
Abuse of my heart
That's just my luck
Yell at me when I'm doing what I should
Snap at me when I'm only doing what I could
Cry to you, man if you only understood
Those high's and low's we bad then we good
I'm trying to talk to you, you never in the mood
I'm trying to work with you, excuse my own feelings just to prove
I'm only trying to love you but you're being so rude
"Man you nagging me, I never do nothing right
This stuff is whack to me, you always wanna fight"
I mean well, my reason is legit
Try to turn it around on me and my feelings seem illegitimate
Am I crazy?, damn is it me?

How dare you have the audacity
To light my love on fire and leave me burning in my own flame
To play a role you never wanted and continue with your game
Give another girl every thing I asked of you

I'm confused
You stopped giving a damn about what I wanted to
And all I get is
"I'm sorry, babe you know I love you. I never meant to do you wrong, I know you mean well, I want you"
Got me on a thin line between I want him,
but he ain't never gonna change
And my heart is weak it beats to your name
I throb at the thought of letting you go
I try to throw my guards up
Taking you back in with my arms up
And find relief in your promises
Then grieve in your absence
It feels like a long distance relationship
I'm here, you're there
All that's between us is a bunch of space and air
Quit doing the things you used to do
Or maybe those were just things I got accustomed to
You reeled me in with your chilvary
Just to get a quick hit and then it all revealed to me
You never put me on a pedestal
You didn't cherish my love
You've forgotten what I've done

Was I not the one
Who kept making sacrifices, kept on compromising
And you, treat me like I was asking too much
When you never budged to change anything for the sake of us
How I took yo sorry ass back when you messed up
Did you forget?
Got me out here looking stupid
And I made my own oath not to fall for another cupid

Damn is it me?
Like how I end up in the same situations
Y'all saying the same damn things on different occasion
It's like I'm digging in the same bowl blindfolded
So I keep choosing you, not that I choose to
Guys keep promising he ain't like the last
Give him a chance, and he leave my ass
I don't think it's true that niggas ain't shit
But it's feeling like "the one" doesn't exist

Ecstasy

Lost in your ecstasy
Playing on my fantasies
Drive me wild
And tell me your wildest dreams

Sweet honey coated chocolate thing
The taste of your majesty;
Excites me, ignites me, entices me;
To help you climb to your peak
See, your lovely drops of medicine;
Is the thing that I seek
Scrumptious sugar almond kisses
Mmmmmm, kiss me
Here, there, everywhere
My thighs to my mid-back
And my ocean rises in compliment
Anticipating the excitement
Yearning for your hardest length
To ease on inside of me
The firm of your touch
Makes all the hairs on my body stand up;
Relieves some sounds of pleasure from my mouth
Begging you for more and more
And you like that sound
The going gets deeper
The going gets strong
My voice a little weaker
I'm saying baby you're so wrong

Lost in your ecstasy
Playing on my fantasies
Drive me wild
And tell me your wildest dreams

The shift has me in control
Yeah, now I'm in control
You relax as I go up and down
Show you like that
When you fight back
With thrusts from your hips
Another, another, another
As we explore all the ways my body contorts
It's a sight to see the way I move in and out of different sorts;
Of positions,
As I beg and you plea
We climb together, yeah both you and me;
Because I was
Lost in your ecstasy
Playing on my fantasies
and you drove me wild
While telling me your wildest dreams

Bodies

I give you myself
In hopes you'd give me you
I slid it all aside just to let you in
It's a poor representation
Of what I have for you
Where's my pride?
I don't know how I lost my prize
Most dignified possession of mine
I lost it every time
Prisoner of my mistakes
I do this time, I cannot shake it
Bag a body, find a replacement
Cause he ain't stay
And excuse my sin to let you in
Find my heart broke in these dead ends
Cause they all end
Repeat behavior
Whose gon' save you
You fucking sucka
You fucking sucka
You fucking, fucked up again
Trade my pain for your pleasure
Do it just to make you better
Make this bed and I lie in it
Cause these sheets won't tell my secrets

Yes, I want this
Yes, I want these worthless minutes for worthless feelings,
worthless attention, from worthless men
as I defy my broken spirit
I put me up and save you some
At request I give you more
I pull my bluff to stop this madness
Would you stay if you didn't have it
And I'm weakened by the truth in your answer

Like The Ocean

My mind is the sea
It runs deep to the ocean floor
And my thoughts drift like the waves
To take a dive into me is a risky thing
The risk of being thrown off course and taken under by my waters
But a beautiful thing when you see all the creatures that swim freely underneath
To have met them is to know the real me

Untitled

I know your ex girl
She is beautiful, too
And I'll never be like her
But I got a feeling
I got to admit this
I might have caught a feeling
And I might have got a little emotional
I shouldn't put myself in this position
Cause I knew what it was
And I tried
But I am just not built to last
I don't know what it is about my heart that gets too attached
I read too much into things
I may have made it what it isn't
I shouldn't put myself in this position
Cause I knew what it was
I know your ex girl
May be nothing like me
That's why you can't feel me that way
You don't see me any way
I am just a common stranger you entertain
I knew what it was
Don't know why I gave it up
I thought it'd be great
Don't know why I got involved
I hate feeling this way
I know you ex girl
A classic can't be replaced
And I am nothing like her

Can't help but compare
Cause I wonder what it was that she did,
Who she was
That made you see her that way
You feel her that way
Feel me?

Pretty Please

They say beauty's in the eye of the beholder
I just wanna know who be holding me
Look at me.
Please tell me what you see
Do you notice me?
Stand in disbelief?
Honestly. I don't see.
Nothing but a silhouette
Just a masquerade
Of lovely.

Pretty, please
Look up to me
Tell it all to me
So I can see

Underdog

I ain't a killa but don't push me, yo
I crack a smile but I'm fed up though
I play pretend like I'm not the greatest
I fall back to do yo ass a favor
Sleeping on myself, I'm mad at myself
How the fuck you mad they don't love you and you don't love yourself
How the fuck you mad? You played yourself.
You mad at the world for a war inside yourself
You ain't bitch made, don't let the world treat you like a bitch man
You don't need no approval and you don't need no applause
And you gone get it regardless even though they pray for the fall
Your light still shines even if they don't see it at all
How many times I gotta tell you?
How many times you gone let these busted niggas fail you cause you like the pretty words they tell you?
You gotta see it yourself
Even when nobody see it you gotta see it yourself
Even when they don't believe it you gotta believe in yourself
Who else?
Gone respect you
Gone protect you
Gone never neglect you
But that reflection
Better give it affection
That's why you love the attention
When you're alone it feels like detention

Yeah, you hear me. You don't listen.
You want love but it ain't in you
Love, everything begins within you
And when you truly understand
What it means to love yourself
You ain't gone need it from a man
When he leaves the pain you feeling now just won't hurt as bad
Yeah, he loved you then but what bout now?
Cant overpower a Queen who owns her crown
Everything they did then they gone think twice now
If I lay the law, everybody'll bow down
And I mean it, I'm about go off now
Ain't taking shit from no bitch nigga I give the pussy the power

The Question

We drift off into space to wonder
Only to return with nothing
But many questions
Forcing pieces to fit
To make some kind of sense of it
And for a moment there is relief
Until the chaos begins again
The attempt to classify truths from points of view
Where in a world of fables it's hard to find a clue
So we sum it up to something counterfeit
'Cause logic won't explain the ambiguous

And what if suddenly you couldn't see your reflection anymore?
Only left to evaluate the within
What would you see, then?
Greetings to my reflection
I admit it's strange to see so closely
Can you envision anything without imagining what it looks like?
Why is that?
Why is death the only invisible thing?
It's the only thing we can't envision clearly
A person is born and can share their life experience with others
A person dies and there's no experience to share
Or is there?
Does the dead know about life?
Why don't the living know about death?
Is it because we all forget?
Because death is so far away from existence

I drift off into space to wonder
Only to return with nothing
But many questions
Forcing pieces to fit
To make some kind of sense of it
And for a moment I find relief
Until the chaos begins again
The attempt to classify truths from points of view
Where in a world of fables it's hard to find a clue
So I sum it up to something counterfeit
'Cause logic won't explain the ambiguous

Answer to The Question

A sweet whisper of a name
To gently awaken the amazing grace
Of something so deep within
I declare I've never witnessed anything more beautiful

Separation

Give me space
Let me breathe
Take a break
I need some peace

I just need some time to clear my mind
I just
I need some clarity
Reality starting to appear in my dreams
I'm feeling all the pain in my sleep

It's hell inside my head
I don't know what to do with myself

Everyday gotta work hard
Everyday wanna be free
Everything gotta be special
Everything gotta be sweet
Fuck that I ain't perfect
I just gotta be me

Hey, It's Our Love Song

I don't gotta mind of my own today
I'm kissing the wind and my thoughts are playin'
I don't know what's real
Am I really here or am I mistaken
Is this just a phase or am I really breakin'
Oh, I'm losing faith
All the memories we're meant to trace
Time is going fast and we gotta race it
Love is spreading but it's not contagious
Leaving all our shadows in awkward places
Oh, I'm holding onto space
I got ugly monsters in my closet
Uninvited, but they don't mean to bother
Their judgment hangs in your honor
If I could just let them walk away
You refuse to visit my dream
Roles can't wear masks in this scene
Jacks will be jacks and kings for queens
This will always be supreme
You don't know how to feel
Curse the dust with gory words
Leave the past undisturbed
Plots and twists left unheard
Keys in holes of knobs unturned
Oh, this is where it all will stay
Ink dried into wet pages
Cause sun didn't come for ages
Faded away in stages
Whispering echoes in closed cages

Oh, now we'll never know
It wasn't hard enough to lose
Disregarded and confused
Wrong don't have a right to choose
Spite is found in me and you
Blinded heart plays a fool
We are both meant to heal

Hades

Deny me?
Try me.
You'll be back before you ever get far
You don't trust the path that leads you blindly
So why you lyin?
You'll let go as soon as you get a grip
And here you'll be at my feet begging me to take you in
You're trying to survive but I'm the one who let you live
Sucks for you don't it?
I know you feel the fire in you burning
You miss it, don't you?
This is an addiction!
You NEED me.
And I'll never let you forget
I know what makes you tick
Love is your temptation
And you'll fall trying to get a taste of it
Once I dangle it in your face…
Ha!
You'll cry to me.
I don't take rejection lightly!!
You'll feel the wrath of my rage at your every escape
No peace shall you find
All the places you attempt to hide in your mind
Hey, I'll be there

I know you feel the weight on your chest
I know under the influence you tend to not think clear
I know the anxiety you get when there's a chance for pain
I know, I know, I know you cry in waves
I keep all your secrets

Do they know?
Ahhh they don't know what they're doing
Should I let them in?
Tell them?
Ehh no need, you'll destruct and I'll gaze at all your beauty
Yeah, you'll be back
You trust me.
In the crevices of your mind you'll find the times we shared in perfect harmony.
Our passion lingers on your lips and nothing in this world will satisfy your cravings the way that I did.

Nostalgia

Nostalgia's here
Reminding me
Of old sadness, old landmarks, old stories
She's making commands to gravity
Pull her down here
She's just a girl living in her dreams
In the clouds somewhere chasing a fantasy
A new something, a new someone, a new feeling
Escaping this reality
Damning the girl she used to be
Nostalgia knows
Who am I
Rings a different tone
No rhetorical question
No great unknown
My mind, body, and my soul
A God child, flower girl, a lion's breath
A heart drenched in gold
An open hand that feeds the birds
A broken curse
The light that rids the shadows
A blossoming rose
A lover's note
The first breath of fresh air
A happy ending of a fairytale

The girl I came to know
Nostalgia creeps and wonders still
Like a fly on the wall
Like raindrops on my window
Like strangers with familiar faces
Persuading me with memories
Of old somebody's, old no where's, old feelings
An invitation to live in an old reality
A bad temptation when nostalgia's here

Poison

My heart wants to tell you I love you even though I know it's absurd. I barely know you even though I feel like I know all I need. Because nothing more or less would erase this curse. No matter how we end up I know you had a beautiful soul. I witnessed you live. I was aware of your flaws. I am. I know. The flaw is me. Your affliction was birthed when you noticed me. Without a sign of caution you continued to pursue this lust. A lust for the broken piece inside of me. A piece you'd get with your tricks and ploys because you knew I'd give you what you were longing for. An invitation laid between my thighs for you to explore the deepest parts of me. There you found all my love letters. Your broken heart needs my broken heart. What a broken mess we are. You knew I'd stare with giddy eyes and burn you with intense affection. A love you never got. I see you. I know you more than you think you know. I wish I could tell you that I loved you while your feet stood firm on the floor. My love may be colored with roses and fantasy. I say that dreams are real too. A choice was made between you and I to live through love and lies. A lie to me and a lie to you that a four letter word is the sum of our worth. I love you enough to say that it's not. It doesn't matter cause it's never enough. And even I display outlandish behavior just to prove it is. I can hear your stupid questions ring like static in my ears. Call it what you please. Just don't say it's poison. When it isn't to me.

Mumbo Jumbo

Look,
It's all right here
I laid it all right here
On the table
In the open
Hands down
Holding nothing
You keep looking down
To see what my hands are holding
Hands up
Talking loud
Clap!
Snap!
Wave.
Can you just look up?
Wow.
You can't see
The callus from the dirt I dug
The pricks from the rose I plucked for you
The scar from the cut I got when I tried to place it in a vase and put it in the window for display

I mean
They're bleeding, open wounds
Vulnerable
Susceptible to disease
Creatures inside prey on my broken flesh
Left me bumpy and bruised
Cramping pain
From the strength I used to carry you
Caress your skin, hold your hand, pray for you
To soothe your beating heart

Sunflower

If you look for a sunflower
Where it doesn't grow
You'll never understand how my petals fold

My flower is rooted in love
The root I give to you

But still you look for more

Reminder: Stay High

I had a daydream yesterday
While I was looking at the sun
I saw myself sitting on a cloud
I was looking down
I saw the rain pour out
I saw the sun go down
I saw the lights go out
I saw the stars
I saw the moon come up
I saw the sun up close
I saw it all
Then I thought about what I witnessed
And I understood

Can't have light without darkness
Can't have healing without pain
Can't have ups without downs
Can't have something without nothing
Can't have loss without gain

I am connected to all the elements of the Earth
That's why I feel so much
That's why I love so deeply
I am in awe at the sight of it
It's a deep knowing I can't explain
A connection like no other
It's within me, deep within me

That's why I speak life through it, to it
Because it's my source
My powerhouse
My God
I was birthed from it
I am made of the dirt
Nurtured by the water
Supported by the sun
Carried by the wind
It is my creator, my family
They are my lovers
God is everywhere
The universe is inside me
In the making of my soul
That's why I daydream about the sun, the stars, the moon
It's why I smell the flowers
It's why I like the rain
It is why I know what I know
I needed and need every element to keep me alive
The water drowns
The sun burns
The wind blows
The sand cuts
Together they shape me and grow me
Everything works together
Cannot have one without another

Inhibition

Inhibition
Please release me
I carry you
Heavy
Like bricks and stones shackled to my feet

Surrender

Here I am
Take me
When I look into your eyes, save me
A subtle invitation
For you to unleash this freak
Untether these lips so they can sing
Untie these hips so they can dance
When I look at you
It's a statement
Clear indication
Of my permission
Yielding to your conviction
Crashing my flesh into yours

Perfect, Imperfection

I undressed my flaws
And laid with you naked
You told me that I was beautiful
But I saw you look away when
You got too close
Did it scare you away
The way they touched you
The scent of it is so strong
Cause my flaws were grown in broken places
That fostered a love so deep
It's hard to fake it
That's how much I loved you
My eyes don't look away
When I saw your scars
I embraced them
But I saw you look away when
I got too close
And it's a shame
Because that's how much you love me
I see you naked

Homecoming

I'm going home again
to recollect my pieces
There are members of myself scattered throughout my hometown
In old houses
In ugly closets
and empty bedrooms
In places that have hid the tears and buried the fears
That lurk in my shadow still
An unpleasant souvenir,
reminding me of a life I wanted to forget
But I've come to reassemble myself
To collect the other parts of me that were left behind
I always wondered where I'd been
and I recently discovered that some of me stayed in places
holding onto hope
that someone would hear my echo
And I hurt when no one came to the door that kept me invisible
But I've come to open it because I care
I care more than they
I love myself that much
That I would face that pain me to find myself at home
A home that didn't nurture my soil with love
for reasons I couldn't know
A home that fostered fear, anger, and shame inside of me
that made it hard to grow
But I've come to gather the pieces of me that are
yearning to be freed
These pieces are mine
and I'm bringing them back with me

And when I leave this place
I will be whole
I would have caressed the declarations of a wounded child's heart
I would have caressed her cheeks
I would have whispered sweetness in her ears
I would have fed her curious mind and fulfilled her wonder
I would have loved her soul
I will cater to these parts of me that were left behind,
and I will give them what they need
I am going home

Forward

Nothing is the same tomorrow
I might lose myself
And I don't care
A piece of me died today

Just a Kid

Everybody gotta dark side
Maybe I should tap into that
Just to get you back
Just to hurt you bad
How you feel bout that?

Don't you test my limits
I might go that far
If you push too hard
Learn from the best after all
You showed me that part
You gave me these scars
You left marks on my skin
These ones still haven't healed on my heart
I was just a kid
Can I vent?

I saw you bruise my mother more often than not
Your hands dug the grave that she slept in long before she died
Your rage was the weapon that triggered me
And your sharp words pierced her body deep
Until she bled all the love she could hold onto for herself and me
And you drained her memory
Every day she forgot again, the woman she was before you
And you called your attachment, love

I was exposed to your brutality
Against my innocent, black, mother
I cried and I begged
Until I choked on my own tears and struggled to catch my breath
We weren't good enough for your mercy

Yet, the same mouth you used to destroy our spirits
Was the same mouth you fixed to complain about police brutality and racial injustices
Because you were tired of living life unfree
And begged for their sympathy
But you were guilty

And I found it strange that you'd call out injustices like these
But turn a blind eye to the violence you perpetrated in your own home
Against black women
Who also wanted freedom from your inability to manage your own ways
You used drugs, alcohol, and violence to cope with your own pains
And that's why I still call you coward because you only act in fear
You'd let yourself self-destruct repeatedly before you ever persevere

And what justice and what peace did we receive?
But broken promises and threats that you would leave
Maybe deep inside you knew your absence was the answer
But the desperate need for love inside of you
Couldn't help but stay and cause disaster

Repeat offender

I haunt you in my dreams
Killed you in my sleep
Murdered the enemy
Fighting wars looking for peace
I was just a kid

Freedom

I am a river
Flowing water
And I will go wherever the current takes me
I am a feather
Lost from a wing
And I will land wherever the wind blows me
I am free
I am a melodic hum in her voice
Full of emotion
And I will go wherever her song takes me
I am the movement in her dance
Effortless motion
And I will let her rhythm lead me
I am free
Or so I believe
I am the spaces between her lips
Words on the brink of disclosure
Soon to be forgotten
Stalling the flow
I am a daydream interrupted
With doubt and question
A lost opportunity to wonder
I am a murmured heartbeat
Sheltered by dense bone
Isolated from synchronicity
I need freedom

The Power of Our Love

Knowledge is power, they say.
And here you are knowing me
Here you are with my words on your tongue and my secrets underneath your clothes
Here you are with my flaws in your eyes
And my love in your hands
Here you are with the book of curses to unlock my past
And a book of spells to break them
Here you are knowing me
Seems as if you've taken control of me
Knowledge is power, they say.
There is power in my vulnerability
I shared with you the experience of knowing me
Knowledge is that of things experienced
And I bet it feels good to hold me
To feel power in the words I spoke into your life that will never leave your lips
To feel the magic of my love boil your soul
To feel like you've known me a thousand years
I bet it feels good to know me
Like you finally got some pussy
Pussy power
There is power in my pussy
And I shared mine with you
Intimately.
I bet it feels good
To hold this pussy high on your pedestal
To let it's glory reign
This pussy is truth explained

You really know it
Knowledge is power, they say
And here I am knowing you
My hands read your hands every time our palms touch, call it palmistry
I study you
I know the places on your body that bring you pleasure and pain
I know which light to switch that could make the shadow go away
I know the strength it took for you to give some of you away
Your power gives me hope
It feels good to hold you
To feel instant relation
To feel a cosmic love combust inside of my constellation
To feel a love that could revolutionize a revelation
The power of our love combined could heal generations
I'm talking about the power of our love, see
Knowledge is power, they say
And you got to know me
I got to know you

Finally

I was shouting on a mountain;
on the edge of losing my breath
Declaring the sky to open
So I could fly up there
Above the clouds
My echoes filled your ears like water
While you were searching the ground for a sign
The quiet you found was so loud
You followed it here
Climbing the mountain that belonged to me
As I stood and surrendered myself to the wind
I died in love when I saw you standing there
Disbelief overcame you
As you witnessed me fly

Colophon

Brought to you by Wider Perspectives Publishing, care of James Wilson, with the mission of advancing the poetry and creative community of Hampton Roads, Virginia.

See our production of works from ...

- Chichi Iwuorie
- Symay Rhodes
- Tanya Cunningham-Jones
    (Scientific Eve)
- Terra Leigh
- Ray Simmons
- Samantha Borders-Shoemaker
- Bobby K.
    (The Poor Man's Poet)
- J. Scott Wilson (TEECH!)
- Charles Wilson
- Gloria Darlene Mann
- Neil Spirtas
- Jorge Mendez & JT Williams
- Sarah Eileen Williams
- Stephanie Diana (Noftz)
- the Hampton Roads
    Artistic Collective
- Jason Brown (Drk Mtr)
- Martina Champion
- Shanya ~Lady S
- Tony Broadway
- Zach Crowe
- Ken Sutton
- Crickyt J. Expression
- Lisa M. Kendrick
- Cassandra IsFree
- Nich (Nicholis Williams)
- Samantha Geovjian Clarke
- Natalie Morison-Uzzle
- Gus Woodward II
- Patsy Bickerstaff
- Catherine TL Hodges
- Jack Cassada
- Dezz
- Jade Leonard

... and others to come soon.

We promote and support the artists of the 757
from the seats, from the stands,
from the snapping fingers andclapping hands
from the pages, and the stages
and now we pass them forth
to the ages

> Check for the above artists on FaceBook, the Virginia Poetry Online channel on YouTube, and other social media.

Hampton Roads Artistic Collective is an extension of WPP which strives to simultaneously support worthy causes in Hampton Roads and the local creative artists.

www.ingramcontent.com/pod-product-compliance
Lightning Source LLC
Chambersburg PA
CBHW021001090426
42736CB00010B/1416